If Kids Ruled the School

More Kids' Favorite Funny School Poems

Selected by
Bruce Lansky

Illustrated by
Stephen Carpenter

ᴍ Meadowbrook Press
Distributed by Simon & Schuster
New York

Library of Congress Cataloging-in-Publication Data

If kids ruled the school : more kids' favorite funny school poems /
selected by Bruce Lansky ; illustrated by Stephen Carpenter.
        p. cm.
Summary: A collection of humorous poems about the trials and
tribulations of going to school.
Includes index.
  ISBN 0-88166-468-5 (Meadowbrook) ISBN 0-689-03273-0 (Simon & Schuster)
  1. Education--Juvenile poetry. 2. Schools--Juvenile poetry. 3.
Children's poetry, American. 4. Humorous poetry, American. [1.
Schools--Poetry. 2. American poetry--Collections. 3. Humorous poetry.]
I. Lansky, Bruce. II. Carpenter, Stephen, ill.
  PS595.E38I36 2004
  811.008'03557--dc22
                                        2003021186

Editor: Bruce Lansky
Editorial Director: Christine Zuchora-Walske
Coordinating Editor and Copyeditor: Angela Wiechmann
Production Manager: Paul Woods
Graphic Design Manager: Tamara Peterson
Illustrations and Cover Art: Stephen Carpenter
Sketch Artist: Jeff Felson

Published by Meadowbrook Press, 5451 Smetana Drive, Minnetonka, Minnesota 55343

www.meadowbrookpress.com

BOOK TRADE DISTRIBUTION by Simon and Schuster, a division of Simon and Schuster, Inc.,
1230 Avenue of the Americas, New York, New York 10020

09 08 07 06   10 9 8 7 6

Printed in the United States of America

Acknowledgments

Many thanks to the following teachers and their students for testing the poems in the book:

Patricia Allegar, East Elementary, New Richmond, WI;
Meredith Andrews, McCarthy Elementary, Framingham, MA;
Diane Clapp, Lincoln Elementary, Faribault, MN;
Hillary Coombes, Deer Creek Elementary, Crowley, TX;
Connie Cooper, Lincoln Elementary, Faribault, MN;
Diane Czajak, McCarthy Elementary, Framingham, MA;
Monica Dailey, East Elementary, New Richmond, WI;
Richard Forrest, East Elementary, New Richmond, WI;
Pamela Greer, East Elementary, New Richmond, WI;
Sandra Kane, Lincoln Elementary, Faribault, MN;
Kathy Kenney-Marshall, McCarthy Elementary, Framingham, MA;
Jenny Myer, East Elementary, New Richmond, WI;
Mary Niermann, Lincoln Elementary, Faribault, MN;
John Pundsack, East Elementary, New Richmond, WI;
Ruth Refsnider, East Elementary, New Richmond, WI;
Cathy Rodrigue, Deer Creek Elementary, Crowley, TX;
Connie Roetzer, East Elementary, New Richmond, WI;
Andrea Rutkowski, McCarthy Elementary, Framingham, MA;
Maria Smith, Deer Creek Elementary, Crowley, TX;
Christy Strayhorn, Deer Creek Elementary, Crowley, TX;
Carleen Tjader, East Elementary, New Richmond, WI;
Pat Towle, McCarthy Elementary, Framingham, MA;
Margie Thell Weiss, East Elementary, New Richmond, WI;
Julie White, East Elementary, New Richmond, WI;
and Cathy Wieme, Lincoln Elementary, Faribault, MN.

Contents

Introduction

If you're among the quarter-million kids and teachers who enjoyed *No More Homework! No More Tests!*, you already know what to expect from this collection of school poems. In case you don't know what to expect, I want to warn you that once you've opened this book, you'll find it very difficult to close.

That pretty much sums up why I write and edit poetry books: I want to write or find poetry so entertaining, you have trouble putting the book down. (You have to close the book in order to put it down—which, as I've already warned you, will be extremely difficult.)

This book contains poems by famous poets like Shel Silverstein, Jack Prelutsky, and Judith Viorst and poems by poets who are becoming well-known because they enjoy visiting schools—including me, Kenn Nesbitt, Ted Scheu, Dave Crawley, Robert Pottle, and Timothy Tocher. (Visit www.PoetryTeachers.com for information about how to invite them to your school.)

Over a thousand elementary students helped me pick the very best poems for this book, and I hope you enjoy reading them as much as those students enjoyed testing them. Better yet, I hope you enjoy reading the poems in this book as much as I do.

Bruce Lansky

Some Bedtime Advice

If tonight when you're in bed
You find it hard to sleep,
Then you should think of happy things
And then start counting sheep.

Then very soon your happy thoughts
Will gently calm your mind,
So when you fin'ly fall asleep
The sweetest dreams you'll find.

But never—ever—think of school.
Oh no! For if you do,
You may start counting teachers
And have nightmares all night through.

Bob Woodroffe

2

Sleep Tricks

I zoomed around at school today
and now, it's time for bed.
My body tells me "nighty-night,"
but what about my head?

My brain won't let me go to sleep,
it's screaming, "Stay awake!"
My mind is racing down a hill,
and guess what? There's no brake.

I'm trying every trick I know
to end this wild ride.
I've looked around for sheep to count,
but they all run and hide.

I think I've found the answer to
my problem for tonight.
I'll get to dreamland faster if
I just turn off my light.

It's working! Now I'm yawning and
the fog is getting deep.
Now if I take my headphones off,
I might just fall asleep.

Ted Scheu

3

The Bus

Sixty kids and one adult,
you gotta love those odds.
The perfect place for pulling pranks
and throwing paper wads.
Hank is standing on his head.
Billy's playing ball.
Peter wet his pants again.
Tasha pushes Paul.
Steven steals. Kevin cries.

Millicent is missing.
Katie punched her cousin Keith.
Ben and Jen are kissing.
Me, I'm taking lots of notes
on public transportation.
I think the bus provides me with
the finest education.

Robert Pottle

4

The Back of the Bus

Oh, the back of the bus is the cool place to hang,
There is lots of loud laughing and often a bang.
There are gestures out windows and whooping and yelling,
And shrieking so shrill that my eardrums start swelling!

The pranks pulled on people when they least expect it
Cause snickering by the emergency exit.
There's stomping and chanting and singing and clapping—
The back-of-the-bus kids directing, arms flapping.

What raucous commotion, like bees in a hive.
But I'm stuck here in front because I have to drive.

Lynne Hockley

Stanley the Fierce

Stanley the Fierce
Has a chipped front tooth
And clumps of spiky hair.
And his hands are curled into
  two fat fists
And his arms are bulgy and bare.
And his smile is a tight little
  mean little smile
And his eyes give a shivery glare.
And I hear that he goes for seventeen days
Without changing his underwear.

But I don't think I'll ask him.

Judith Viorst

6

The Toughest Boys in School

Don't mess with us! Don't be a fool!
We are the toughest boys in school.
So if you meet us—best behave.
We're big and strong and very brave.
Though I admit it's true to say
That we've been known to run away
From kids at school who call us names,
Who laugh at us and spoil our games.
'Cause even though we boys play rough,
The girls in school are twice as tough.

Bob Woodroffe

Mrs. DeBuss

Our second-grade teacher, named Mrs. DeBuss,
has never had such a fun classroom as us.
You see, all the students have interesting names
instead of just plain ones, like Sarah or James.

So when she calls roll it is terribly funny,
she calls "Lauren Order" and then "Xavier Money."
Then "Ben Dare" and "Dawn Datt" and "Isabel Ringing,"
"Amanda B. Reckondwith," "Ella Fantsinging."

She calls "Cole Doubtside," "Anna Won," "Anna Tu,"
"Justin Time," "Justin Case," "Ahmal Wright," "Howard Yu."
She calls "Noah Liddle" and "Isaiah Lott"
plus "Diane Tumeechu" and "Heywood U. Knott."

"Claire Skyes" and "Paige Turner" and "Mike Carson-Fire."
"Jack Hammer," "Paul Barer," "Ed Hertz," and "Barb Dwyer."
Then "Colin Alcars," "Moira Less," and "Les Moore,"
"Sonny Day," "Sandy Beach," and then "Robin D. Store."

She calls "Woody Dewitt" and "I. Betty Wood,"
"Jose Ken Yusee" and then "Willie B. Goode."
She calls "Marcus Downe" and the "Natalie Drest,"
and lastly, of course, she calls "Olive D. Wrest."

Kenn Nesbitt

Class Pest

The boy who sits behind me
Is really, really mean.
He tells me I have cooties and
I smell like a sardine.
He tries to steal my pencils
And my favorite crayons, too.
I wish his folks would move away
And lock him in the zoo.
He cheats on every spelling test
And blames it all on me.
He always pulls my ponytail.
I wish he'd let me be.
He talks too loud, his laugh is weird.
I wish that he were mute.
But the worstest thing about him is…
          I think he's kinda cute.

Kathy Kenney-Marshall

I Wonder If She'd Like Me

I wonder if she'd like me if I stood a little taller.
I wonder if she'd like me if my ears were only smaller.
Or maybe if I brushed my hair and gave her a red rose,
or if I changed my underwear and didn't pick my nose.
Perhaps if I could ride a mule. Perhaps if I could dance.
Perhaps if I could come to school in polka-dotted pants.
Perhaps if I would shine my shoes and even wear a tie,
or if I wrestled kangaroos or sang a lullaby.
Or maybe if I built a ship and sailed the seven seas
with nothing but a paper clip and tubs of cottage cheese.
I wonder if she'd like me for the reasons I have listed.
I wonder if she'd like me if she knew that I existed.

Eric Ode

12

Katie Kissed Me

Katie kissed me! Yuck, it's true!
My face took on a greenish hue.
My knees, like jelly, started shaking.
Then my stomach started quaking.
Slobber slithered down my cheek.
My consciousness was growing weak.
My ears were ringing, head was spinning.
But all the while Kate was grinning.
My heart was pounding through my shirt.
My tongue felt like I just ate dirt.
Though you may think I've lost my brain,
I wish she'd kiss me once again!

Christine Lynn Mahoney

13

Bad-Hair Day

I looked in the mirror
with shock and with dread
to discover two antlers
had sprung from my head.

The kids in my class
were complaining all day,
"We can't see the board
with your horns in the way!"

The teacher was cross.
He asked, "What's your excuse?"
I said, "Well, I think I have
used too much mousse."

Linda Knaus

14

Missing Something?

When I got dressed for school today
I was not quite awake.
I put on shoes that do not match—
An innocent mistake.
My socks, I fear, are not the same;
One's blue, the other's red.
My underwear is...
Oh, good grief!
I'm going back to bed!

Mary Jane Mitchell

I Ripped My Pants at School Today

I ripped my pants at school today
while going down the slide.
It wasn't just a little tear
I ripped 'em open wide.

Now everyone at school can see
my purple underwear.
Although the sight makes people laugh
I'm glad I've got them there.

Robert Pottle

17

I Should Have Stayed
in Bed Today

I should have stayed in bed today,
in bed's where I belong,
as soon as I got up today,
things started going wrong,
I got a splinter in my foot,
my puppy made me fall,
I squirted toothpaste in my ear,
I crashed into the wall.

I knocked my homework off the desk,
it landed on my toes,
I spilled a glass of chocolate milk,
it's soaking through my clothes,
I accidentally bit my tongue,
that really made me moan,
and it was far from funny
when I banged my funny bone.

I scraped my knees, I bumped my nose,
I sat upon a pin,
I leapt up with alacrity,
and sharply barked my shin,
I stuck a finger in my eye,
the pain is quite severe,
I'd better get right back to bed
and stay there for a year.

Jack Prelutsky

Why Dju I Dju zha Shings I Dju?

Why dju I dju zha shings I dju?
Why djon't I ushe my head?
I should have sheen it coming;
I should have shtayed in bed.
Inshtead I'm in zha clashroom,
and zha day izh quite a mesh.
My teesh are shtuck togezher,
and itsh my fault, I confesh.
I mushed have been dishtracted
azh I walked in shrew zha door.
I put my booksh upon my chair
and shat down on zha floor.
I shtuck my crayons to my feet
and colored wish my shoe.
I put my milk inshide my deshk,
and zhen I drank my glue.

Eric Ode

Cursive Curse

My *m*'s are much too bumpy.
My *u*'s are far too lumpy.
My *k*'s are way too droopy.
My *l*'s are all too loopy.
My *e*'s are *i*'s, and *i*'s are *e*'s.
My *z*'s have got some rare disease.
My *y*'s are tilted to the right.
My *x* is not a handsome sight.
My wimpy *r*'s are worst of all;
the bumps on top are much too small.

My pencil shouts to stop for air.
My hand is sore. This isn't fair!
My teacher doesn't understand.
I'll never have a steady hand.
I feel a need to scream—or worse.
So close your ears, 'cause I might curse.

Ted Scheu

Work with Me

Artwork is for artists.
Brush- and framework, too.
Groundwork's for reporters—
That's what they must do.

Fireworks are to celebrate.
Teamwork helps in sports.
Needlework's for tailors.
Casework is for courts.

Footwork is for dancers.
Handiwork for moms.
Metalwork for craftsmen.
Clockwork goes in bombs.

Paperwork's for writers.
Techwork is for nerds.
Woodwork is for carpenters.
But homework's for the birds!

Mary Jane Mitchell

21

Fs Are "Fabulous"

Hey, Mom and Dad! I got my grades!
And you'll be thrilled to hear
the marks on our report cards
are changed around this year.

A bunch of kids were telling me
this morning on the bus,
that they had heard some teachers say
that Fs are "fabulous."

And Ds are proudly given out
for work that's "dynamite."
They're used to honor kids like me,
whose brains are really bright.

So C of course is super "cool"—
I've got a few of those.
I wish they could be Ds and Fs,
but that's the way it goes.

I'm pleased to see my teacher
didn't give an A or B.
I've worked too hard for one of those.
Gosh, aren't you proud of me?

I see you don't believe me.
You think that I am lying?
At least you will agree
that I should get an A for trying!

Ted Scheu

Testing, Testing, Testing!

Testing, testing, testing!
They're testing us to death.
At school, we take so many tests
we're almost out of breath...

From testing, testing, testing!
It's all we seem to do.
If you could look inside our brains,
you'd see they're black-and-blue...

From testing, testing, testing!
And that is my concern.
We take so many tests each week
there's never time to learn.

Ted Scheu

School Rules

Do not oversleep and miss the school bus—
you'll be late.
That's a habit teachers generally
don't appreciate.

Never tell your friends at school
that you still wet your bed.
They are sure to tease you,
and you'll wish that you were dead.

Never call your teacher a name
when she's not near you.
Teachers' ears are excellent,
so they can always hear you.

Do not read a textbook when your hands
aren't clean—it's tricky
to separate the pages when the pages
get real sticky.

When you go out for a team
it's always wise to practice.
When you're a substitute,
the bench can feel like cactus.

Do not copy homework from a friend
who is a dummy.
If you do, I'm sure that you
will get a grade that's crummy.

And if your report card's bad,
don't blame it on your buddy.
Kiss up to your parents quick,
or they might make you study.

Bruce Lansky

25

Homework

What is it about homework
That makes me want to write
My Great Aunt Myrt to thank her for
The sweater that's too tight?

What is it about homework
That makes me pick up socks
That stink from days and days of wear,
Then clean the litter box?

What is it about homework
That makes me volunteer
To take the garbage out before
The bugs and flies appear?

What is it about homework
That makes me wash my hair
And take an hour combing out
The snags and tangles there?

What is it about homework?
You know, I wish I knew,
'Cause nights when I've got homework,
I've got too much to do!

Jane Yolen

The Aliens Have Landed!

The aliens have landed!
It's distressing, but they're here.
They piloted their flying saucer
through our atmosphere.

They landed like a meteor
engulfed in smoke and flame.
Then out they climbed immersed
   in slime
and burbled as they came.

Their hands are greasy tentacles.
Their heads are weird machines.
Their bodies look like cauliflower
and smell like dead sardines.

Their blood is liquid helium.
Their eyes are made of granite.
Their breath exudes the stench of foods
from some unearthly planet.

And if you want to see these
sickly, unattractive creatures,
you'll find them working in your school;
they all got jobs as teachers.

Kenn Nesbitt

Get Out of Bed!

"Get out of bed, you silly fool!
Get up right now, it's time for school.
If you don't dress without a fuss,
I'll throw you naked on the bus!"

"Oh, Mom, don't make me go today.
I'm feeling worse than yesterday.
You don't know what I'm going through.
I've got a strange, rare case of flu.

"My body aches, my throat is sore.
I'm sure I'm knocking on death's door.
You can't send me to school—*achoo!*—
'Cause everyone could get it, too.

"Besides, the kids despise me there.
They always tease and always stare.
And all the teachers know my name.
When something's wrong, it's me
     they blame."

"You faked a headache yesterday.
Don't pull that stuff on me today.
Stop acting like a silly fool—
The principal cannot skip school!"

Diane Z. Shore

30

Falling Asleep in Class

I fell asleep in class today,
as I was awfully bored.
I laid my head upon my desk
and closed my eyes and snored.

I woke to find a piece of paper
sticking to my face.
I'd slobbered on my textbooks,
and my hair was a disgrace.

My clothes were badly rumpled,
and my eyes were glazed and red.
My binder left a three-ring
indentation in my head.

I slept through class, and probably
I would have slept some more,
except my students woke me
as they headed out the door.

Kenn Nesbitt

How to Torture Your Students

Start each day with a surprise quiz.
Don't dismiss the class for recess
until you've finished the lesson
you're working on.
At the end of the day, hand out a huge
assignment that's due the next day.

When a student says, "I have to go to
the bathroom," say, "You should have
gone this morning before you left
home" or "You'll have to hold it in;
it's time for the kindergarten to use
the bathrooms."

Never call on students who have
their hands up.
Only call on students who have
no idea what's going on.

When a student asks you a question,
say, "Look up the answer in a book."
Don't bother to mention the name
of the book in which the answer
can be found.

When you read, go as fast as you can.
Skip a line or two, then ask questions
about the passage to see if the
students were listening.

When it's time for the students to
read, call on someone who doesn't
have a book.

When you hand out pencils, make sure
they're dull and don't have erasers.
When you hand out books, make
sure they're torn and tattered.

When preparing the students for a test, write all the information they'll need to know on the board. Then stand in front of the board so they can't see what you've written. As soon as you've finished discussing the test information, turn quickly and erase the board.

On the last day of school, hand out a surprise final exam.
Tell your students if they flunk it, they'll have to attend summer school—and if they flunk summer school, they'll have to repeat the grade.
Tell them you hope they all flunk because you like them so much and you wish they could be your students again next year.

Jane Pomazal and Bruce Lansky

My Excuse

This morning I was walking
past the local county jail
when I was captured by a pirate
just released on bail.
He took me to his pirate ship
and taught me how to sail
and made me wed his daughter,
who was covered by a veil.
We sailed the seven stormy seas
through hurricane and gale,
but while we were marauding,
we were swallowed by a whale.

We soon escaped by torturing
the whale with a nail
and floating to the shoreline
in an empty wooden pail.
An Indian then guided us
along a western trail
and led us to a stagecoach
that was carrying the mail.
We all delivered letters
through the sleet and snow and hail,
until we found a train,
and then we rode upon the rail.
I barely made it back to school
to tell you of my tale.
I'm sorry that I missed the test;
I hope I didn't fail!

Kenn Nesbitt

I Will Not Tease Rebecca Grimes

I have to write one hundred times:
"I will not tease Rebecca Grimes."
Okay, that's one. I'm far from done.
(This isn't gonna be much fun.)

"I will not tease Rebecca Grimes."
That's two. I'm paying for my crimes.
It's all because I pulled her hair
And put spaghetti on her chair.

Because I gave her goofy looks
And squirted mustard on her books,
I have to write one hundred times:
"I will not tease Rebecca Grimes."

That's three. Whoopee. It's going slow.
Just ninety-seven more to go.
"I will not tease" (I'm keeping score.)
"Rebecca Grimes." (Now that makes four.)

I'm soaked with sweat. My shirt is damp.
I think I'm getting writer's cramp.
"I will not, will not, will not tease
Rebecca Grimes!" Can I stop, please?

The teacher frowns, and that means no.
I still have sixty-six to go.
"I will-will-will not-not-not-not
Tease-tease-tease-tease..." It's getting hot.

"I will not tease Rebecca Grimes."
That's ninety-nine. The school bell chimes.
Just one more line and I'll be through.
Rebecca Grimes, this one's for you!

My final line will rhyme with "Grimes":
"I will not tease Rebecca...Slimes!"
Rebecca Slimes! Ha ha! That's great!
I'd better hide it. Oops! Too late!

The teacher sees what I wrote down.
She takes my paper with a frown.
I now must write one thousand times:
"I will not tease Rebecca Grimes."

Dave Crawley

I Call First!

"I call first to get a drink! And first to eat my snack!
I call first to go to gym, and first when we come back!

"I call first to leave for lunch! And first to switch the light!
I call first to read out loud the poems that I write!

"I call first to sharpen up my pencil, loud and slow!
And when we get to sharing time, I call first to show!

"I call the computer! I call the special chair!
And I call first in line each time that we go anywhere!

"And on the hill at recess, I get to be the king!
I call first forever and for every little thing!"

I said those things in class today until my teacher heard.
She sat right down and made a list to keep me at my word.

So now I'm first to dump the trash and sweep the silly floors.
I'm first to be the last in line—'cause I hold all the doors.

I'm first to wipe the tables off and scrape off clods of clay.
I'm first to pass the paper out and put the paints away.

I'm first to stack the stupid chairs and first to scrub the sink.
I'm prob'ly not the first to see that being first can stink!

Ted Scheu

My Teacher Pays Me to Be Good

My teacher pays me to be good,
Which I think is okay.
I get a dollar every time
I'm good for one whole day.

Whenever I behave myself
For one entire week,
He pays me twenty bucks and I'm
So happy I can't speak.

If I act proper for a month,
My teacher is so nice.
I get a hundred dollars for
My noble sacrifice.

And now my teacher says that if
I'm good throughout the year,
I'll get a trip to Disneyland.
It's lots of fun, I hear.

My teacher's sold his car and moved
Out of our neighborhood.
He's running out of money,
But our class is really good.

Pat Dodds

Lucky Trade

I told my mom I'd go to work
if she would go to school.
She thought that trading places once
just might be kind of cool.

So she agreed; I packed her lunch
and made her wash her face.
Then Mother said, "I wonder why
you want to take my place?"

"I wonder what you do at work.
I'd like to meet your boss.
Now hurry up and brush your teeth
and don't forget to floss.

"There's just one other thing, Mom,
that I forgot to mention:
I'll pick you up at four o'clock—
today you have detention."

Matthew M. Fredericks

45

My Pencil

The pencil that I nibble on
Looks funny with its color gone.
I chewed off every bit of paint;
It once was yellow—now it ain't.

Its roughness lends a steady grip,
Which means my hand will rarely slip.
And such are its distinctive looks,
That everybody knows it's Cook's.
So if I've dropped it carelessly,
It always gets returned to me.

Alas, we're at that fateful day:
My pencil must be thrown away.
I've used it well—there's just a stub,
A wee eraser-headed nub.

I love it when I buy them new—
When I unwrap a Number 2.
With sharpened point and glossy sheen,
Its future's filled with words unseen.
And then (I feel I must confess),
I sniff its wondrous woodenness.

Is this the pencil I'll respect?
The one my chompers won't affect?
Can I control this nasty habit?
Perhaps, for once, my teeth won't grab it.

My pencil had such perfect paint;
It once was yellow...now it ain't.

Christopher Cook

Stupid Pencil Maker

Some dummy built this pencil wrong—
The eraser's down here where the point belongs.
And the point's at the top—so its no good to me.
It's amazing how stupid some people can be.

Shel Silverstein

Gym Class

The locker room smells nasty,
And my gym shoes smell like feet.
My socks smell like they're made of cheese
Or spoiled rotten meat.

The toilets are all backed up,
And the floors are soaking wet.
The stench around the benches
Is from everybody's sweat.

The shower stalls are moldy.
All the uniforms are stiff.
The air reeks of deodorant;
I dare you—take a whiff!

I'm not the smartest person,
But I know this much is true:
Instead of calling it P.E.
It should be called P.U.

Neal Levin

The Monkey House

Our teacher said, "I have some news
About our local zoo.
The Monkey House is empty—
All the monkeys have the flu.

"And so until they're better
And can gibber, scream, and chase,
The zoo and I have both agreed
You kids can take their place."

Bob Woodroffe

The Day the Dinosaurs Come Back

The day the dinosaurs come back,
there's bound to be a big attack.
I bet they stomp upon the schools;
bedevil teachers; act like fools;
upset the slides; break all the swings,
the monkey bars, and climbing rings.
And when the grownups run and hide,
they'll kneel and give us kids a ride.

Timothy Tocher

My Doggy Ate My Homework

"My doggy ate my homework.
He chewed it up," I said.
But when I offered my excuse
My teacher shook her head.

I saw this wasn't going well.
I didn't want to fail.
Before she had a chance to talk,
I added to the tale:

"Before he ate, he took my work
And tossed it in a pot.
He simmered it with succotash
Till it was piping hot.

"He scrambled up my science notes
With eggs and bacon strips,
Along with sautéed spelling words
And baked potato chips.

"He then took my arithmetic
And had it gently fried.
He broiled both my book reports
With pickles on the side.

"He wore a doggy apron
As he cooked a notebook stew.
He barked when I objected.
There was nothing I could do."

"Did he wear a doggy chef hat?"
My teacher gave a scowl.
"He did," I said. "And taking it
Would only make him growl."

My teacher frowned, but then I said
As quickly as I could,
"He covered it with ketchup,
And he said it tasted good."

"A talking dog who likes to cook?"
My teacher had a fit.
She sent me to the office,
And that is where I sit.

I guess I made a big mistake
In telling her all that.
'Cause I don't have a doggy.
It was eaten by my cat.

Dave Crawley

The Best Show-and-Tell

Today I'm first for show-and-tell.
I brought it in a box.
I hoped that it would be the best—
No boring toys or rocks.
I took my box up to the front
And slowly raised the lid.
I pulled it out and held it up…
Then Teacher ran and hid.
The kids began to run and squeal.
I couldn't understand.
The skunk I held was small and cute.
It jumped down from my hand.
It went to greet the kids in class,
Who scattered left and right.

And when LuAnn let out a screech,
I guess it got a fright.
Its tail went up, out came a spray,
An odor filled the air.
Then kids and things went flying fast,
One tripped upon a chair.
The room was empty in a flash.
I guess they couldn't wait
To tell their moms and dads the news—
My show-and-tell was great!

Wendi Silvano

54

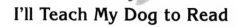

I'll Teach My Dog to Read

I'll teach my dog to read.
I'll teach my dog to write.
He'll multiply in record speed.
He'll learn to be polite.

I'll teach my dog the golden rule,
and he'll be so well-bred,
next year I'll send my dog to school,
and I'll stay home instead.

Eric Ode

Ollie's Escape

Ollie escaped in the classroom,
And that was an awful mistake.
It would have been folly
To try to catch Ollie,
Since Ollie's a seven-foot snake!

He wiggled his way toward the teacher,
Who jumped on her desk with a scream.
Faster and faster
He squiggled right past her.
Old Ollie was picking up steam!

The rest of us ran for the closet
As Ollie slid right out the door.
We heard a loud squall
As he entered the hall.
He's a difficult snake to ignore.

He slithered his way to the office,
As teachers jumped out of his way.
But Principal Poole
Is the boss of the school—
We wondered just what he would say.

It didn't take long for an answer.
In fact, he decided to scoot.
He burst through the door
With a terrified roar
And a seven-foot snake in pursuit.

Ollie the snake was excited,
And we, of course, thought it was fun
To see teachers hiding
While Ollie was sliding
And Principal Poole on the run.

They ordered us out of the building,
And somebody called the police.
There were doctors and vets
And men with big nets
To make sure the problem would cease.

But Ollie, at last, was exhausted.
He snaked his way back to his den.
When they searched all around,
He was finally found—
Curled up, asleep, in his pen.

Dave Crawley

To Our Missing Classmate—Get Well Soon

Disasters keep on happening
   Because you are not here.
The intercom is broken, so
   Announcements are not clear.

The principal got measles and
   The teachers got the flu.
The students all have chickenpox,
   The janitor turned blue.

The roof blew off the schoolhouse and
   The grounds all flooded, too.
Well, no, we made the whole thing up
   But, really, we miss you!

Susan Reade Smith

I Gave My Teacher a Present

My teacher got a present
she thought was really cool.
She got it when I had the flu
and missed a day of school.

Maria Smith

Dot-to-Dot

I've got a red dot on my nose.
I've got two 'tween my eyes.
I've got eleven on my head
and twenty on my thighs.

And on my back there's eighty-one,
If Daddy counted right.
I've even got ten on my rear.
It's not a pretty sight.

I thought I had the chickenpox.
My mother thought so, too.
But last night I discovered
That's entirely untrue.

My sister took Mom's laundry pen.
Into my room she crept.
And with that pen she scribbled
Loads of red dots while I slept.

And though I do not have the pox,
These red things really fool
My mom and dad and teacher,
Who won't let me back in school!

Kathy Kenney-Marshall

A Sick-Day Trick

I didn't want to go to school,
and so I played a trick.
I coughed and wheezed and
  blew my nose
so Mom thought I was sick.

I slowly walked downstairs and lay
across the kitchen table.
When Mom said, "Sit up straight,"
I sighed, "I would, if I were able."

She looked at me a bit surprised
but felt my cheeks and head.
I told her I'd feel better
if I read a book in bed.

Mom sort of laughed, but soon agreed
to keep me home. Hooray!
There's just one thing that I forgot—
today is Saturday!

A. Maria Plover

Cafeteri-Yuck!

It's broccoli mush and strawberry slush
With vegetables mashed up and stewed.
I'd rather lick dirt from the sleeves of
   my shirt
Than eat cafeteria food.

It's easy to tell from the frightening smell
Today won't be much of a treat.
There's warmed-up tomatoes and
   soggy potatoes
To go with the mystery meat.

I'm avoiding the pork while sticking
   my fork
In the side of a slippery beet,
Which swims in a river of leathery liver
And gravy that's unfit to eat.

If I were marooned on the side of
   the moon,
I think that I still would conclude:
I'd rather chew rocks and sweaty
   old socks
Than eat cafeteria food.

Dave Crawley

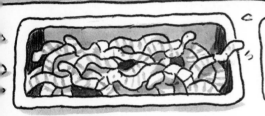

Tray Trouble

I remember the day I bobbled my tray.
It fell to the floor with a smash.
With a clank and a clatter, I saw my
     food scatter,
And everyone jumped at the crash.

It was silent at first. That part was
     the worst.
Then laughter broke out with a roar.
They hollered and howled. They
     yammered and yowled
As I stared at the food on the floor.

I just have to confess, I had made
     quite a mess.
My lunch was a mountain of goop.
And my face was as red as the beet,
     which had spread
To the ice cream and vegetable soup.

I had hoped that I might simply van-
     ish from sight
As I wiped up the floor with a rag.
I thought, "Never again." And ever
     since then,
I've brought my own lunch in a bag.

Dave Crawley

But First...

I had a bit of trouble
With my teacher yesterday.
She said I had to get to work—
There wasn't time to play.
But first...
I had to tie my shoes.
I had to blow my nose.
And then I had to clean the lint
That tickled 'tween my toes.
I had to find my pencil,
Had to sharpen up its tip.
I had to zipper up my pants,
Then Vaseline my lip.

And then, of course, 'cuz it was cold
I put my sweater on,
Then found a new eraser 'cuz
My old one was all gone.
And then I found a buggy bite
I really had to itch.
And scratching made me notice
That my sweater pulled a stitch.
And so I pulled a little thread.
I made a little hole
And noticed that my elbow had
A tiny brownish mole.
It looked just like a ladybug,
And so I drew a nose.
I added spots and little legs
And teeny buggy toes.
Then fin'ly with those things all done
I settled down to work.
But all my friends had finished,
And my teacher went berserk.
And, really, I was so confused.
I wasn't having fun.
These things were quite important.
They were begging to be done!
So now it's time for science.
We're on page ninety-four.
But first...
There are some markers I must pick up
    from the floor...

Kathy Kenney-Marshall

I Pledge Allegiance

I pledge allegiance to the floor,
the walls and ceiling, classroom door.
I pledge allegiance to my books,
to desk and papers, coat-rack hooks.
I pledge allegiance to my bag,
to Joni's pigtails—and the flag.

Timothy Tocher

The Third-Grade Christmas Play

My mother drops me off at school.
I shout, "Hooray! Hooray!
Today's the day I'm starring in
the third-grade Christmas play!"

I'm all decked out like Santa Claus
and looking kind of weird.
I'm dressed in red from head to toe
with mustache, wig, and beard.

There's rouge upon my cheeks and ears
and also on my nose.
I'm patting on my belly
while I practice ho-ho-ho's.

I'm wearing big black rubber boots,
a shiny leather belt,
and soft white winter mittens
that my mom cut out of felt.

I'm ever so embarrassed,
asking friends for clothes to borrow.
I just found out the Christmas play
is not until tomorrow.

Linda Knaus

68

Credits

Author Index

Title Index